CHANGE YOUR LITERACY CHANGE YOUR LIFE

Begin Your Personal FINANCIAL REVOLUTION

A Stop Being a Sucker® Book

Tom MATHEWS | Kim SCOULLER | Andy HORNER

howmoneyworks.com

For more information: licensing@wealthwave.com.

Creative direction, design, and production by Andy Horner and the WealthWave® Team. Cover Design: Andy Horner

wealthwavemedia.com

To everyone who dreams of knowing the potential of money...

With every page, you'll redefine the boundaries of what's possible. Remember, the power of financial literacy is not just in reading these words—it's having more control of your world.

This journey is a testament to your ambition and desire for growth. By increasing your literacy, you don't just change the direction of your life—you define the destination.

May this book be a compass to guide you as you embark on your financial transformation. May it be your true north as it points you to this truth: **If you can change your literacy, you can change your life.**

Let's get to work...

Featuring The Cast of TheMoneyBooks Series

Clark - 36, Rideshare Driver

He has a "brilliant" idea for an app if he could just raise enough cash... from anyone who wants in on the dream. Until then, it's the rideshare thing. Flexible hours. No cubicles. Captive audience. What's not to love?

Dana - 42, Hospital Director

Smart and energetic, Dana is the kind of high performing executive everyone wants to be in the room with. Everyone except those who aren't doing their jobs. Why? Because they all know Dana doesn't play.

Sarah - 49, Real Estate Agent

Some may forget to dot their i's and cross their t's, but not Sarah. Especially not in the word "stickler." While not known for tact, Sarah's honesty and persistence have helped her remain a top producer for over a decade.

TJ - 32, Medical Sales

TJ was made for sales and sales were made for TJ. He's got the only infectious things any doctor would ever want in their office—a deadly smile and a killer personality.

Mei - 56, History Professor

Mei's students all share two fond memories from her class. Her favorite expression: "It's possible to be both nice and precise." And "Jeopardy Day", when the students get to be contestants and Mei gets to be Alex Trebek.

Hector - 28, Restaurant Owner

A born motivator, Hector runs a small fleet of food trucks. Social media made his sandwiches a city-wide success, which is why he named the business "Social Sandwich."

Zoey - 19, University Student

Zoey can't decide between physical therapy or marine biology. The choice would be simpler if people were as appreciative as animals when you do something nice for them. And by "people," she means her roommates.

George - 67, Retired Military Officer

Civilian life suits George well. Aside from restoring the old Mustang, he Facebooks with friends, FaceTimes with family, and facepalms over today's teens, who could all benefit from a butt-kicking bootcamp... in his opinion.

Contents

Introduction

Financial illiteracy is a terrible vulnerability. Easily exploited, it's how many opportunities in life are lost and how possibilities for the future are missed. It's the unlocked door that enables those who know how money works to steal the American Dream from their fellow Americans.

For past generations, enjoying the American Dream didn't require financial literacy. All you needed was to work hard for your employer and pay taxes. With these two contributions, you could buy a car and a house big enough for your family and a comfortable pension and social security check for retirement.

Today, however, few employers provide pensions, and the future of social security is uncertain. This leaves Americans responsible for protecting themselves financially and building their wealth and legacy for the future.

The hope of financial independence and security is now the responsibility of each of us. In other words, your financial future is up to you.

And that's a major problem. Here's why...

The majority of Americans are financially illiterate and have been so for generations. This is largely because we have depended on schools, corporations, and the government as a safety net. And the truth is, they prefer that people remain ignorant about money—because when we are clueless about money, taking advantage of us is easy. We'll sign up for high-interest credit cards, spend our paychecks on things we don't need, leave our money in low-interest savings accounts, and pay unnecessary taxes. Financial illiteracy has made easy pickings of Americans—who, for the most part, only know how to earn a paycheck and spend it. That's what happens when people don't understand how money works.

When your financial literacy is low, your economic opportunities and future can be stolen by those who know everything about money and have all the financial power—the banks, the credit card companies, the marketers, the corporations, and the government. They are the American Dream thieves.

So how DO we take back the American Dream?

From the title of the book, I'm guessing it's financial literacy.

That's right, George and Dana. Financial literacy is the only way.

When you change your financial literacy, you're changing the rules of the game. Becoming financially literate enables you to literally take control of your money, your potential, and your future from the hands of those who were counting on you remaining a sucker.

To alter your future, you must gain financial knowledge. This will empower you with a lifelong foundation for growth, security, and prosperity.

In this book, we'll delve deep into the startling realities that underline the state of financial literacy in the United States. From schools to households, teenagers to retirees—the ripple effects of a nation's financial illiteracy touch every corner, every age, and every socio-economic class.

Amidst the alarming statistics, there are tales of triumph–stories of individuals who hoisted themselves from the pit of financial despair with ropes of information and knowledge. This book is as much a reflection of the current state of the financial crisis as it is a beacon of hope.

We'll walk through the hallways of U.S. schools where students are starved of financial education and prepped for a life of financial mistakes. We'll examine the gap between what's not taught and the education crucial for our children to thrive in an increasingly competitive and complex financial landscape.

We'll explore the heart-wrenching cost of financial ignorance and be inspired by tales of redemption—showing it's never too late to learn. Moreover, we'll discover that you don't have to go on this journey alone.

“

A trusted financial professional can be like a compass in the vast, often turbulent sea of financial decisions.

The expertise you'll gain from these stories is a lifeline and a bridge from where you are to where you aspire to be. You'll discover that you can reclaim your American Dream and transform your financial well-being and destiny with the proper financial knowledge.

Are you prepared to challenge your perceptions and, most importantly, empower yourself?

All it takes is changing that one, tiny facet of your life to reshape your financial reality—your literacy. Let's embark on this journey together to empower a nation, starting with you.

CHAPTER 1

Echoes of a Crisis

The Current State of Financial Literacy in America

In the heart of San Diego...

Laura, a recent graduate with a good job at a prestigious firm, stared down at her mounting credit card bills. The numbers didn't make sense. Years of higher education had armed her with knowledge on diverse subjects, but when it came to understanding her finances, she was, to put it mildly, perplexed.

In front of her friends, during the numerous business meetings she attended, Laura appeared to have everything together. However, behind closed doors, her finances were a mess.

Laura's story is not unique. It is an echo of a nationwide crisis. From the bustling streets of major cities to the quiet corners of small towns, millions of Americans find themselves in a similar predicament. They may be earning decent money, but they lack the understanding about how to manage, save, and grow their wealth. They're trapped in a cycle of living paycheck to paycheck, borrowing more than they can repay, and saving less than they ought to.

Tom Mathews' CPA father said,

"It's not how much money you make, but how much money you keep and how hard it works for you."

These words resonate with profound truth. Wealth isn't just about earnings. It's about financial discipline, understanding, and literacy. It's about making every dollar work and, more importantly, making it work for you.

Recent studies paint a grim picture. A significant number of American adults admit to not sticking to a budget.[2] Many can't handle a sudden $400 emergency expense without borrowing or selling something.[3] Even more alarming is that most are functioning with a poor level of financial literacy and find it difficult to handle retirement planning, mortgage decisions, or everyday spending choices.[1]

> **The answer, Sarah, is complex and multifaceted.**

A system that thrives on credit, an educational framework that doesn't prioritize financial learning, and a society that often equates success with possessions all play their roles. But pointing out the culprits won't solve the issue. Recognizing the gravity of the situation and taking collective responsibility might.

If Laura, with her college degree, finds herself drowning in the turbulent waters of financial instability, what hope do others have? Laura's story is a reflection of a systemic flaw. But there's hope. Movements are taking shape all across America. Schools are beginning to recognize the importance of financial education, nonprofits are stepping up to bridge the gap, and individuals are seeking knowledge.

In the grand scheme of things, the story of Laura and countless others serves as a wake-up call. Addressing financial literacy isn't about pointing fingers or laying blame. It's about understanding the importance of having the proper financial knowledge. It's about ensuring that all of us have the tools not just to earn but to save, invest, and build a legacy for future generations.

In early 2024, 25 states guaranteed a personal finance course for all public high school students.[4] Eight states have fully implemented their program, and 17 are in progress. Other states, like Arizona, may offer a personal finance or economics course, but it's not currently guaranteed.

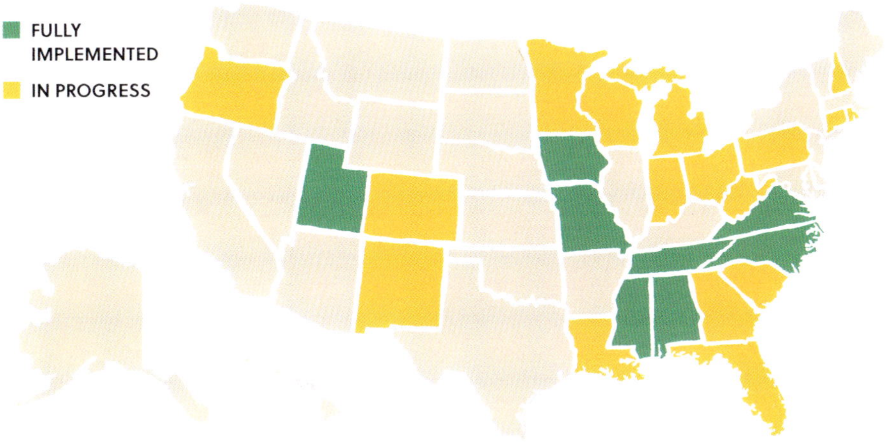

To see how your state is doing in terms of K-12 financial education, go to "The Nation's Report Card," which gives each state a grade from A to F.[5]

An improvement from 8 states to 25 states in 4 years shows that a revolution is coming, and we're proud to be a part of it. It's a call to action, and we urge you to join us in this journey toward a financially literate America. Let's invest in our future and empower individuals, families, and communities to take control of their finances. Because financial literacy isn't just about numbers—it's about freedom, confidence, and building a better tomorrow for all.

> **An investment in knowledge pays the best interest.**
>
> — BENJAMIN FRANKLIN

CHAPTER 2

Foundations and Fallacies

Financial Curriculum in U.S. Schools

Within the four walls of his classroom...

Marcus, a dedicated high school teacher, has witnessed countless moments of epiphany among his students. The joy of understanding a complex algebraic formula or discussions about Einstein's theory of relativity often fills the room. But one day, during a casual conversation about future aspirations and dreams, Marcus encountered a glaring blind spot: his students, for all their academic brilliance, were woefully unprepared for the real-world financial challenges that awaited them.

The issue wasn't their intelligence or capability but the absence of financial education from their curriculum. One of his students remarked, "Why do I need to know about compound interest when I'm going to be a doctor?" This question struck Marcus hard, and he realized the urgent need for financial literacy in schools. Schools excel at laying down foundations in science, arts, and the humanities. Still, they often miss imparting critical knowledge about money, saving, investing, and understanding the financial decisions of daily life. This neglect is a fundamental flaw in preparing our youth for adulthood.

Nelson Mandela once proclaimed,

"Education is the most powerful weapon you can use to change the world."

True to these words, education shapes perspectives, builds character, and equips us with tools to transform our lives. Shouldn't our educational institutions also prepare students with the financial knowledge required to navigate the real world? Unfortunately, our academic education has been incomplete.

Marcus recognized this yawning gap. Instead of waiting for the system to change, he decided to be the change. He began organizing weekly financial literacy workshops, bringing in local financial experts to discuss budgeting, taxes, investments, and loans. The response was overwhelming. Students were hungry for this knowledge, eager to grasp concepts directly affecting their futures. Many admitted they'd often felt lost during family discussions about money, mortgages, or college costs. Now, they felt empowered and equipped with information to make wiser decisions.

Parents, too, began to take notice. They opened up and shared their stories of financial pitfalls, wishing they'd received this kind of education during their formative years. Many acknowledged that they learned about money the hard way, through mistakes and poor judgement, because no one had taught them otherwise. Privately, a few parents even confided their ongoing challenges with debt and financial strain, wishing their children to avoid making similar missteps.

The importance of introducing financial education in schools cannot be overstated. When we ignore this, we send students into the world with academic knowledge but without the tools to manage one of life's most crucial aspects: money. We unintentionally expose them to potential hardships, such as overwhelming student loans, credit card debt, inadequate retirement planning, and unnecessary strain on their significant relationships.

But the solution is within reach. Incorporating financial literacy into the curriculum helps to better prepare our students for the challenges ahead. We now know that home or personal experiences are not enough to teach children about money. While these play a role, a structured educational approach is essential. Our children don't learn math or literature solely through family interactions, so why should financial literacy be any different?

Marcus' initiative powerfully illustrates the pivotal role our schools play in reshaping the financial future of the next generation. We must revise our educational system's blueprints to equip our students for the future. It's not just about grades; it's about providing them with the knowledge to lead financially secure and prosperous lives.

> **"**
>
> **Carpe diem, seize the day, [boys and girls], make your lives extraordinary.**
>
> —JOHN KEATING (PLAYED BY ROBIN WILLIAMS), DEAD POETS SOCIETY. DIRECTED BY PETER WEIR

Now, more than ever, we must seize the day to ensure the next generation is equipped with a complete academic education that includes financial literacy skills they need to make their lives truly extraordinary.

CHAPTER 3

The Steep Price of Ignorance

Tales of Financial Woes

Amid the bustling streets of Dallas...

Rosa, a resilient single mother of two, balances many daily roles—from being her children's loving caregiver to working long hours at a local diner. Beyond her roles, Rosa battles a silent enemy: the snare of payday loans that have steadily entrapped her.

Rosa's story began with a single loan, taken out in desperation to cover an unexpected medical bill for her youngest. With limited financial understanding, the promise of a quick solution seemed like a lifeline. But, as weeks turned into months, she found herself trapped in a cycle of borrowing, with accumulating interest charges that seemed insurmountable. Each loan became another chain, adding weight to her already heavy burden, with no clear end in sight.

Unfortunately, her story is not uncommon but rather represents the experiences of many individuals nationwide. The world of finance, with its complicated fine print, remains a mystery to a lot of people. Understandably, these financial products appeal to people—who wouldn't want early access to their paycheck to cover immediate expenses? However, within this lack of understanding lies numerous dangers. From exploitative lending practices to misguided investment schemes, the repercussions of financial illiteracy can be devastating, often exacting a toll far more significant than any of us can fathom.

As the saying goes,

"The cost of ignorance is far higher than the cost of education."

As Rosa's situation illustrates, the repercussions of not understanding financial intricacies can lead to choices that compound problems rather than solve them. In addition to losing money, it takes a mental and emotional toll, causes stress, and brings a sense of helplessness that comes with it.

In a new survey, 52% of respondents listed money as the #1 stressor that is taking a toll on their mental health.[6]

But why does this ignorance prevail?

One reason is the absence of accessible financial education for all. Many grow up without being taught the basics of budgeting, the perils of high interest loans, or the benefits of saving. As a result, we are more susceptible to making decisions that offer short-term relief but long-term hardships when faced with financial challenges.

Though fraught with challenges, Rosa's journey also became a beacon of hope. Witnessing her struggles, a neighbor introduced her to a local financial literacy workshop. There, Rosa began to unravel the complexities of her decisions and learn the tools to navigate her way out of debt. The road was long, but armed with knowledge, she began to break free from the shackles of her loans, one payment at a time. Rosa harnessed the power of debt-reducing strategies such as the Snowball Method and budgeting. She started on a long-term savings plan to secure her future. Step by step, month by month, Rosa and her children broke free from the gravitational pull of her debt, forging a path toward financial freedom.

Her tale is a poignant reminder of the need for widespread financial education. It's not just about numbers and calculations but about empowering each of us to make informed decisions, understand the consequences of our choices, and build a stable foundation for our futures.

Rosa's story and countless others like hers are compelling narratives on the steep price of financial ignorance. But they also inspire hope. They underscore the transformative power of knowledge and taking action based on what you learned. We've seen the challenges, either in our own lives or the lives of people close to us. Now is the time for all of us to step up and take action.

The 2022 Financial Literacy Annual Report of the Consumer Financial Protection Bureau (CFPB) details the CFPB's financial literacy strategy and activities to improve consumers' financial literacy.

cfpb Consumer Financial Protection Bureau

https://files.consumerfinance.gov/f/documents/cfpb_financial-literacy-fy-2022_annual-report_2023-03.pdf

Understanding the actual cost of ignorance strengthens our resolve, inspires us, and spurs us to invest in the greatest asset of all: knowledge.

"Learning is a treasure that will follow its owner everywhere."

– CHINESE PROVERB

CHAPTER 4

Turning the Tide

Success Chronicles from Financial Education

Amid the looming skyscrapers and bustling streets of Chicago...

James stood at a precipice. A few years earlier, he had been a confident entrepreneur, riding the waves of his budding startup. However, a series of poor investment decisions and a lack of understanding about financial management had pushed him to the brink of bankruptcy. For James, the descent was not just monetary but emotional, filled with sleepless nights and the constant dread of an uncertain future. His personal financial situation was in a shambles as well. Like many entrepreneurs and business owners, James reinvested every penny he earned back into his company, leaving him with no personal savings or safety net.

But, like all great tales, James's story did not end in despair. Instead, it was a beginning, a testament to the transformative power of financial education.

It began with a chance encounter at a local cafe, where he overheard a discussion on financial topics. The conversation between a financial educator and her student was a revelation. It occurred to him that while he had entrepreneurial skills, he lacked foundational knowledge about managing and growing wealth. Determined to turn his life around, he decided to learn how money really works.

Over the next year, James immersed himself in books, workshops, and websites. From understanding the basics of debts and investments to figuring out the nuances of taxes and savings, he rebuilt his financial knowledge from the ground up. The transformation was palpable. As he applied his newly acquired insights, he began restructuring his business to reduce unnecessary expenses and invest more. Moreover, he paid attention to his personal financial situation, allocating a portion of his earnings as emergency funds and retirement savings. He even started a financial education program within his company, sharing the knowledge he had gained with his employees.

The tide had genuinely turned for James. Within a few years, not only did he pull himself out of impending bankruptcy, he also achieved what many dream of: financial resilience. His business flourished, and so did his wealth. More importantly, the constant fear and anxiety that had plagued him were replaced by confidence and serenity.

Sharon Lechter once said,

"Financial freedom is freedom from fear."

Before he learned how money works, fear governed his decisions—the fear of loss, the fear of the unknown, the fear of failure. But knowledge equipped him with the tools to navigate through rough waters and calm seas, allowing him to make informed choices and chart a course toward success.

Before I started my food truck business, I had a failed restaurant that ruined me financially. Talk about despair! It was knowledge that 'de-fanged' the fear and got me back on my feet. It took a few years, but knowing there was a way back with education changed my mindset to hope.

Thanks for sharing, Hector. Like James's recovery, that's an inspiring story of financial redemption.

James's story serves as a beacon of hope for many. It underscores the undeniable fact that no matter how dire the situation, you can pivot toward a brighter future with the proper education and mindset. Financial literacy is more than understanding numbers and charts. It's a springboard for empowerment, autonomy, and the freedom to dream without monetary constraints. As we reflect on success stories like that of James, we recognize the profound impact of financial education. It's a life skill and a lifeline, a beacon that can guide us from the darkest depths towards the sunlit shores of financial well-being and security.

James's transformation from the edge of despair to the pinnacle of success is inspirational and instructive. It is a potent reminder that challenges can be overcome with determination, resilience, and proper knowledge, no matter how impossible they seem. As we navigate the waters of finance, let us remember that financial literacy can be the wind in our sails, steering us away from treacherous storms and toward brighter horizons.

As we ride the waves of finance, we can take inspiration from the words of the legendary surfer:

"We're all equal before a wave. We're all wiped out equally. It's the perfect balance.

– LAIRD HAMILTON

CHAPTER 5

Money Basics

Core Principles Every American Should Know

In a cozy living room bathed in the soft glow of the afternoon sun...

Anna sat down with her young granddaughter, Lily. Surrounded by a lifetime of memories captured in photo frames and mementos, Anna felt a pressing responsibility. As she approached the twilight of her life, she wanted to ensure that Lily, with the vast expanse of her future ahead, had the wisdom of financial principles that Anna had learned, often the hard way.

Anna began with a story from her twenties. Fresh out of college and starting her first job, she was giddy with the excitement of her first paycheck. But without understanding how money works, she spent frivolously, saved inconsistently, and avoided investments due to fear of the unknown. Decades later, Anna wished she had known to make more informed financial decisions.

Anna shared the timeless tenets she wished someone had taught her:

Live Within Your Means

Before building wealth, you must develop discipline. No matter how much you earn, spending more than you make will always lead to financial instability.

The Power of Compounding

Start saving early, even if it's a small amount. Over time, with the magic of compounding, your savings can grow exponentially.

Avoid Debt

While some debts, like mortgages, can be seen as investments, avoiding unnecessary liabilities is essential. High interest debts, especially from credit cards, can be financially crippling.

Pay Yourself First

Make saving a priority. Set aside a portion of your income before paying bills or buying non-essential items. It's easier to save consistently when it becomes a habit.

Invest Wisely

Understand the basics. It's not about chasing quick riches but about steady growth over time. Diversify your accounts and never put all your eggs in one basket.

Emergency Fund

Life is unpredictable. A safety net in terms of savings can be the difference between a minor setback and a financial catastrophe.

Education is Continuous

The financial landscape evolves. Commit to lifelong learning, staying updated with changes in the financial world.

As Anna spoke, she could see the curiosity in Lily's eyes. The young girl was like a sponge, absorbing every word and understanding the value of these lessons, not just for herself but for the generations to come.

To drive her point home, Anna quoted an old Chinese proverb:

> **"The best time to plant a tree was 20 years ago. The second best time is now.**

She wanted Lily to understand that while we can't change the past, the future is a blank slate. Anna hoped her financial regrets would serve as a lesson, a roadmap to guide Lily on a path Anna wished she had taken.

Their heart to heart talk ended with a promise. With the wisdom of her grandmother's experiences, Lily pledged to apply what she learned and pass it on, so the future generations of their family would stand on a solid financial foundation.

My parents and grandparents were scholarly, but they never shared financial wisdom with me as Anna did with Lily.

A good financial professional can give you that wisdom today, Mei.

Anna's conversation with Lily underscores the critical importance of financial education. While the market may go up and down and investments may change, certain core principles remain timeless. Wherever you are in your life, it's imperative to remember that it's never too early or too late to start your financial literacy journey. Regardless of past mistakes or missed opportunities, there's no better day than today to take control of your financial destiny.

> **Someone is sitting in the shade today because someone planted a tree a long time ago.**
>
> —WARREN BUFFETT

CHAPTER 6

Crafting Financial Futures

Navigating Finances from Student Life to Adulthood

Amid the sprawling campus of UCLA...

Rahul, a sophomore majoring in economics, was already planning his financial future. Peers surrounded him, many reveling in the newfound freedoms college life afforded. While most were busy making weekend plans or contemplating which courses to choose, Rahul wasy busy studying spreadsheets, interest rates, and long-term goals.

Rahul's journey began during his high school years. He watched his older cousin grapple with the weight of student loans, the pressure to repay overshadowing the joy of graduation. Determined not to fall into a similar trap, Rahul made it his mission to be proactive about his finances, starting with his student loans.

He began by looking for scholarships and grants, spending countless hours researching and applying. By the time he started school, a significant portion of his tuition was already funded through these efforts. Rahul chose a federal student loan with a clear repayment plan for the remaining balance.

Rahul then expanded his financial knowledge to better understand savings and investments.

He took Warren Buffett's words to heart:

"Do not save what is left after spending, but spend what is left after saving."

With this mantra, Rahul set up an automatic savings system, diverting some of his part-time earnings into a savings account paying a higher interest rate.

Moreover, understanding the Time Value of Money concept, Rahul dipped his toes into the stock market. With the help of a financial professional, he invested in a diversified portfolio, focusing on long-term growth rather than short-term gains. He also sought internships at financial firms, keen on applying what he was learning in school to the real world.

Rahul's friends often looked at him with both admiration and puzzlement. Their initial impression of him was that he was years older, even though they were all the same age. It wasn't just his focus on finances but also how he clearly understood his future and the steps needed to achieve it. For many, adulthood felt like a distant horizon, with immediate experiences taking precedence over future planning. But Rahul was unyielding in his belief that the foundation for a secure financial future was laid during these crucial college years.

As his senior year approached, while most students were anxious about impending student loan repayments, Rahul was already several steps ahead. His meticulous planning helped ensure that he was prepared for loan repayments and had a nest egg of savings and a growing investment portfolio. Instead of graduating with a sense of impending financial doom, Rahul felt confidence and optimism.

To learn from Mr. Overachiever, Rahul, should I find a financial professional while still a student? How do I do that when I'm so young?

Your parents, a trusted friend's parent who knows about money, a professor from the business school, or the person who gave you this book are all excellent places to get a recommendation, Zoey.

Rahul's story stands as a powerful testament to the importance of early financial planning. Transitioning from student life to adulthood can be rife with challenges, with many finding themselves unprepared to handle the daily financial decisions in a grown-up world. However, this transition can be smooth and immensely rewarding with foresight, education, and proactive measures.

Crafting a prosperous future for yourself requires a blend of knowledge, discipline, and vision.

Core Elements to Begin Your Financial Journey

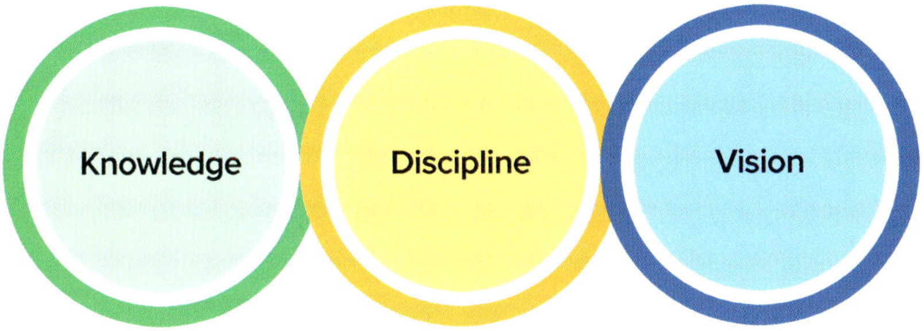

While it's easy to get lost in the immediacies of present-day life, especially during the transformative college years, it's essential to remember that the future is just around the corner. And being prepared for that future, as Rahul's journey highlights, begins with the big and little decisions you make today.

> **"It's not how much money you make, but how much money you keep, how hard it works for you, and how many generations you keep it for.**
>
> –ROBERT KIYOSAKI

CHAPTER 7

Mastering the Dollar

Strategies for Successful Money Management

Lucy had always been a dreamer...

From spur of the moment travel plans to her aspirations of owning a quaint bookstore, her dreams were as colorful as they were vast. However, every time she thought about taking the steps to turn her dreams into reality, her finances or the lack of money held her back.

In her early twenties, Lucy's wanderlust and the allure of credit cards landed her in a pool of debt. She was living beyond her means, juggling multiple credit card bills with high-interest rates and struggling to make ends meet. The once carefree girl had become consumed by anxiety and fear of financial ruin.

The story isn't unfamiliar. Like many, Lucy had plunged into the world of credit cards, tempted by immediate gratification, only to find herself sinking deeper into the quicksand of debt. Monthly bills piled up, interest rates soared, and soon, her once-shiny credit cards were chains that shackled her dreams.

One evening, while sifting through a mountain of bills and trying to make sense of her dwindling bank balance, Lucy stumbled upon a quote by Dave Ramsey:

"A budget is telling your money where to go instead of wondering where it went."

That was a big aha for her. "You mean, I can control my money instead of it controlling me?" she muttered to herself. She realized that her free spirit needed some structure regarding money.

Determined to change her narrative, Lucy embarked on a journey to master her finances. Her first step was creating a budget. She categorized her expenses, identified areas of unnecessary spending, and set limits. Dining out was reduced, online shopping curtailed, and non-essentials like magazine subscriptions and some streaming services were canceled. She committed to using only cash for an entire month to break her habit of excessive credit card spending.

Next, Lucy tackled her debts. She adopted the Snowball Method, targeting smaller debts first for quicker wins, which motivated her to keep at it. As each debt was paid off, the money that was previously allocated for its payment was directed into clearing more significant debts.

Lucy also recognized the importance of an emergency fund. Starting with a small goal, she gradually saved up enough to cover three months' expenses, ensuring that unexpected events wouldn't derail her financial progress. She put it in a separate account, so she wouldn't be tempted to use it for non-emergencies. This approach allowed her to access the funds when she needed them without making it *too* easily accessible.

But budgeting and saving weren't enough. Lucy knew she had to make her money work for her. She began educating herself about investments. From reading books, watching online videos, and attending seminars to seeking advice from financial professionals, Lucy learned the basics of stocks, bonds, and mutual funds.

The original book, "HowMoneyWorks: Stop Being a Sucker," has a chapter called "Build Wealth." It's one of the 7 Money Milestones and it helps you make sense of making your money work for you. It's AWESOME!

Education and then action. That's the power that Lucy harnessed. Slow and steady action with knowledge is how you build wealth—and you're right, Hector—that book is a great resource.

Slowly but steadily, the tide began to turn. From drowning in debt, Lucy became financially savvy, watching her debts diminish and her investments grow.

Years later, as she stood in her bookstore, enveloped by the smell of freshly printed pages, Lucy's once-distant dreams now felt within reach. She was ready to transform those dreams into reality, all without the burden of financial debt.

Lucy's journey is a powerful lesson about taking control of your finances. Often considered too complicated to understand, money can be simplified with the right strategies. Mastering it isn't just about escaping debt or accumulating wealth; it's about the freedom to make your dreams come true and carving out a path for your aspirations.

Money is a crucial tool in the grand tapestry of life, where dreams and ambitions shine as the brightest threads. It can either constrain or empower, depending on how it's managed. And as Lucy's story underscores, taking control of your money, directing it with purpose and vision, is the first—and perhaps the most pivotal—step towards a brighter, more prosperous financial future.

"Wealth isn't about having a lot of money; it's about having a lot of options."

- CHRIS ROCK

CHAPTER 8

Investing in Tomorrow

The Power and Potential of Forward-Thinking Finance

Bo had always been a man of humble origins...

With hands toughened by years of labor and a spirit undeterred by the daily grind, he'd worked tirelessly in the city's shipyard. Each morning, as the sun cast a golden hue over the vast expanse of the harbor, Bo would begin his routine, surrounded by the cacophony of machines and the relentless rhythm of the docks.

However, beneath that blue-collar exterior lay a sharp, analytical mind that understood the power of foresight. While his co-workers spent their wages in the present, Bo always invested for tomorrow.

One evening, as Bo sat with a group of fellow workers, the topic of retirement came up. Many were concerned about their financial future, unsure if their modest savings would be enough. Bo, however, had a different perspective. He talked to them about his investments, the little amounts he'd started putting away in his younger days, which had grown considerably.

Drawing inspiration from the wise words of economist Paul Samuelson, Bo had always believed that,

"Investing should be more like watching paint dry or watching grass grow. If you want excitement, take $800 and go to Las Vegas."

For Bo, investing was never about quick riches or the latest trends. It was about patience, research, and understanding the market's ebb and flow. He understood that, like gardening, investing required constant nurturing and tending. And just like a garden, it could yield an abundant harvest when given enough time and care.

Bo began with small investments in mutual funds. Over time, as he learned more about different asset classes, he diversified his portfolio, including stocks that promised steady growth. He also ventured into bonds and real estate, ensuring multiple avenues for his money to multiply.

Different Asset Classes

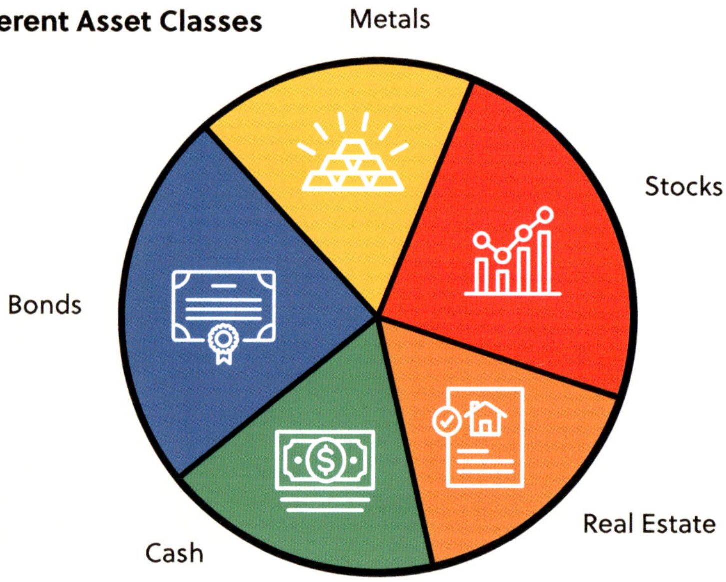

The Real Key to Bo's Success—Consistency!

He didn't let market fluctuations deter him. Even when the economy faltered or stocks plummeted, Bo held on, keeping his eyes firmly on the long-term horizon. And his persistence bore fruit. By the time he was ready to retire, Bo had secured a comfortable life for himself and created a legacy for the generations to follow. Despite his modest lifetime income, the remarkable power of compound interest had a profound impact, steadily growing his investments over time.

Bo's story highlights the power of forward-thinking finance. Long-term investments may seem old-fashioned or dull in a world increasingly driven by instant gratification and TikTok trends. Yet, as Bo's journey shows, the potential of this steady approach is the best way to accomplish your goals. It's not about being wealthy or having extensive financial knowledge. It's more important to understand the value of time, the magic of compound interest, and the rewards of patience.

In essence, the finance landscape is vast, and while there might be multiple paths to wealth, the route of long-term investment stands out for its stability and assurance. While the present moment holds its charm, the smart move is investing in the future and planting seeds that can provide a bountiful harvest.

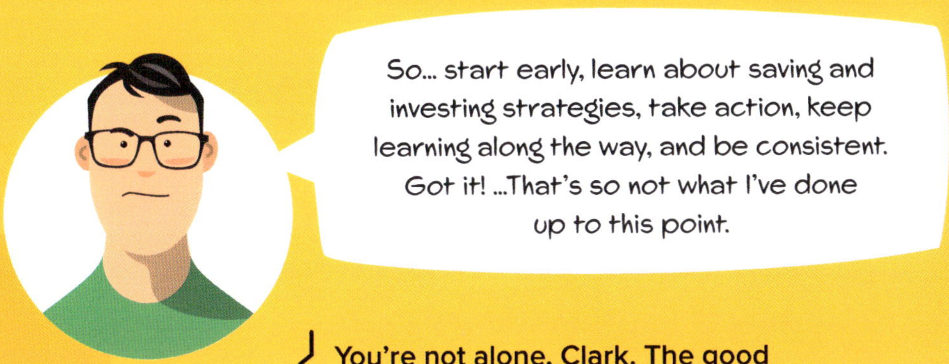

You're not alone, Clark. The good news is you can get started today.

The future, with all its uncertainties and mysteries, rewards those who patiently, consistently, and wisely invest in its potential. Investing isn't just a financial decision. It's a step towards reaching your financial goals. However, it's vital to recognize that we need not sacrifice the present for the sake of the future. By embracing forward-thinking finance, we can savor the best of both worlds.

> **"**
>
> **All we have to decide is what to do with the time that is given us.**
>
> — GANDALF, 'THE LORD OF THE RINGS, THE FELLOWSHIP OF THE RING'

CHAPTER 9

Passing the Torch

Financial Literacy's Multigenerational Impact

In the small town of Evergreen...

the Harrison family was well-known, but not for the reasons one might think. Their story, a saga spanning three generations, is a testament to the transformative power of financial literacy.

The tale begins with Robert Harrison, a hardworking man whose life, in many ways, was dictated by financial uncertainty. Raised during the Great Depression, Robert had a firsthand understanding of scarcity. Despite working tirelessly, he struggled to make ends meet, often living paycheck to paycheck. Without financial training or guidance, he did not know how to manage, save, or invest his earnings.

Robert wanted more for his son, John. Recognizing the gaps in his education, he enrolled John in a local financial literacy program. John grasped these lessons eagerly, internalizing the teachings of wise budgeting, the importance of saving, and the fundamentals of investing.

Guided by the words of Epictetus,

"Wealth consists not in having great possessions, but in having few wants."

With a disciplined approach to his finances, John avoided needless debts, made wise investments, and crafted a comprehensive long-term financial strategy.

Under John's stewardship, the fortunes of the Harrison family began to flourish. Their journey to prosperity was driven by resilience and determination. The once formidable concept of 'risk' in business and investing became familiar and well-managed. Where Robert faced challenges, John thrived. As he established his own family, he passed on these values to his daughter, Katie.

Katie Harrison represented the epitome of her family's financial evolution. With the combined wisdom of her grandfather's experiences and her father's teachings, she navigated the world of finance with an ease that would have been unimaginable for her grandfather. Entrepreneurial and savvy, she expanded the family's wealth, helping to ensure her financial security and setting the stage for future Harrisons to thrive.

But Katie's most profound legacy wasn't just in the assets she amassed but in the knowledge she passed on—it was education for her community. She regularly hosted financial workshops in Evergreen, so that her community, especially the young people, had the tools to make informed financial decisions.

The story of the Harrisons is a tale of monetary success and the transformative impact of financial education. From Robert's struggles emerged John's determination, and from John's prudence blossomed Katie's prosperity. Their journey underscores the importance of financial literacy and its potential to break cycles of economic hardship, replacing them with legacies of growth and stability.

The Harrison family story shows us that financial education can empower you to take control of your destiny, to make informed decisions, and to help ensure that the lessons learned are passed on, creating a ripple effect of prosperity.

As we consider the multigenerational impact of financial literacy, one thing becomes clear: knowledge is the most valuable asset we can bestow upon our successors—the torch that lights their way, the shield that protects them from adversity, and the foundation on which they build their dreams. When we arm the next generation with financial wisdom, we help secure their present and we fortify their future.

“Just as a candle cannot burn without fire, generations cannot thrive without wisdom passed from the old to the young. When knowledge flows across generations, it illuminates a path, sparking an enduring legacy of prosperity.

– TOM MATHEWS

CHAPTER 10

Digital Empowerment

How Modern Technology is Shaping Financial Education

In the digital age...

the pace at which information travels and the tools at our disposal have reshaped countless aspects of our lives, and financial education is no exception. As financial landscapes become increasingly complex, the role of technology in simplifying and demystifying money matters cannot be overstated. Where there was once a lack of access to financial resources and knowledge, technology has bridged the gap and empowered individuals like never before.

Enter Michelle. A thirty-something graphic designer, Michelle always considered herself fairly savvy with her finances. However, a sudden job loss put her in an unforeseen predicament. She felt cornered with bills mounting and her savings depleting faster than anticipated. Rather than succumb to despair, Michelle saw this as an opportunity. She decided to harness the power of technology to rebuild her financial life.

Beginning with a thorough online course on budgeting and savings, Michelle familiarized herself with the basics she'd previously overlooked. She explored digital platforms that automatically categorized her expenses, giving her a clear overview of her spending habits. These insights, though initially jarring, were transformative. She realized that while earning well, her spending patterns were unsustainable. The amount she earned was not as important as the amount she saved, as the numbers at the end of the month truly told the story.

Next, Michelle ventured into the world of digital investments. She started diversifying her portfolio through online trading platforms, focusing on long-term growth. She became a regular on financial education webinars, tapping into a global community of experts and peers who shared their knowledge and experiences. Michelle joined the Loud Budgeting movement, making her finances and financial goals public on social media.

Perhaps most crucially, Michelle used tech-driven networking platforms to freelance, tapping into the gig economy on the weekends. This provided her with a steady income stream, diversified her skills, and expanded her clientele.

> **“**
>
> **Technology is nothing. What's important is that you have faith in people.**
>
> — STEVE JOBS

And it was true for Michelle. While the digital tools at her disposal were instrumental, her resilience, willingness to learn, and faith in her abilities reshaped her financial world. Her journey reinforced a fundamental concept: financial empowerment is about understanding and implementing sound money management practices, creating multiple income streams, and constantly growing one's knowledge base. Technology augments these efforts by providing unprecedented access to information and resources.

Today, Michelle's story is not unique. Across the globe, countless individuals are leveraging technology to enhance their financial literacy. From apps that teach kids about savings to platforms that guide retirees through investment decisions, technology is democratizing access to financial education.

With all the advancements technology brings, the heart of financial success is based on timeless principles: spend less than you earn, invest wisely, and always plan for the future. Technology, in all its glory, serves as a magnifier. It can amplify good habits but also highlight poor decisions.

As we navigate the 21st century, the harmonious melding of traditional financial wisdom with modern technological tools will be the key to success. Michelle's story illustrates that while technology can be a powerful ally in our financial endeavors, the foundation remains rooted in understanding and applying core financial principles. As we lean into the future, technology can multiply our efforts, but the heartbeat of financial literacy remains unchanged.

> **It takes 20 years to become an overnight success.**
>
> — EDDIE CANTOR

CHAPTER 11

Building Bridges

Encouraging Collaborative Efforts in Communities and Schools

Community and education are the twin pillars of growth and progress in any thriving society...

But what happens when these pillars join forces, especially concerning financial literacy? What could be accomplished if the entire community works together to tackle economic hardship?

Deep in the heart of a midwestern town, residents faced a familiar issue. High inflation, rising unemployment, and resulting financial strain eroded the town's vibrancy. For many, fundamental financial principles remained a mystery. Debts were mounting, savings were dwindling, and hope was scarce.

However, change began with a simple realization: the power of collective action. Led by a group of concerned parents, educators, and local business owners, the town decided to tackle its financial literacy problem head-on. Their goal was clear—to educate every member, young and old, on how money works. But their approach had to be unique, engaging, and community-driven to succeed.

Local schools began to integrate financial education into their curriculums. Classes weren't limited to just students. Eager to learn, parents, grandparents, and community members filled classrooms in the evenings. Business owners offered internships and workshops, helping residents understand the practicalities of commerce, profit, and savings. Employers held financial planning seminars for their employees, empowering them to take control of their future.

But education wasn't limited to the four walls of a classroom...

Town Gatherings
turned into financial literacy workshops.

Local banks and credit unions
provided resources, seminars, and one-on-one counseling sessions.

The Community's Public Library
dedicated a section solely for financial education, with books, online courses, and a monthly guest speaker series.

The ripple effects of this collective effort were profound. Not only did individuals become more adept at managing their finances, the entire community began to flourish. Debts were reduced, savings grew, and a newfound financial confidence permeated the town. With practical knowledge, students made wiser choices about further education and career paths. Adults, no longer burdened by financial uncertainty, began to invest in local businesses, further invigorating the economy.

In the words of Helen Keller,

"Alone, we can do so little; together, we can do so much."

The town's story exemplifies how collaborative efforts can amplify impact, turning challenges into stepping stones for broader success.

But perhaps the most beautiful part of this journey was its self-perpetuating nature. As one generation became financially literate, they automatically became ambassadors of this knowledge, passing it on to the next. This multigenerational transfer of wisdom ensured that the lessons learned would not fade but become an intrinsic part of the community's fabric.

While financial literacy greatly benefits the individual learner, it's a community's treasure. When we recognize the power of collective action and the strength of unity, we can transform not just individual lives but entire communities. Just as bridges connect distant shores, united efforts in communities and schools can bridge the gap of financial education, leading to a brighter, more secure future for all.

"

Coming together is a beginning, keeping together is progress, working together is success.

— HENRY FORD

CHAPTER 12

Trusted Guidance

The Essential Role of Financial Professionals

Navigating the complex waters of finance often feels like getting lost in a maze...

The multitude of choices, the weight of decisions, and the fear of mistakes can be overwhelming. In this vast landscape, one beacon stands out as invaluable: the guidance of a trusted financial professional.

Carla was no stranger to these challenges. A talented aerospace engineer, her income was decent, and her life was comfortable. Yet, her financial picture was clouded with doubts. Savings seemed non-existent, investments were a puzzle, and planning for the future? It felt like a distant dream. "How is it that I can build rockets, but I can't seem to make sense of my own finances?" Carla thought, frustrated and confused.

She had attempted to chart her path, reading books and using online tools. But the maze only seemed to grow more complicated. Encountering a multitude of conflicting ideas, she found herself in a state of confusion. Who could she turn to for help? It wasn't until a close friend recommended seeking help from a financial professional that Carla considered another approach.

Hesitant but hopeful, Carla met with a financial professional. Their initial conversation was a revelation. They didn't focus on numbers or which stocks to invest in. The majority of the conversation centered on understanding Carla's dreams, values, and fears. The financial professional listened intently, providing a safe space for her to express her concerns and ask questions. This holistic approach combined the art of understanding individual aspirations and the science of financial planning to provide a personalized roadmap for success.

Weeks turned into months, and the changes were palpable. With the professional's insights, Carla streamlined her expenses, optimized her savings, and began investing intelligently. The confusion of retirement plans, insurance, and taxes became straightforward with expert guidance. Not just a better financial status, Carla also achieved peace of mind, knowing she was on a path tailored for her success.

Warren Buffett's wisdom fits this situation,

"The best investment you can make, is an investment in yourself."

The benefits of clarity, strategy, and growth made the time spent with a financial professional worthwhile. Her decision to meet with a licensed professional was an investment in her future, which could result in monetary returns and the intangible return of confidence and security.

Yet, Carla's story is not an isolated case. It mirrors the experiences of countless individuals who recognize the difference between wandering in the financial wilderness and walking a defined, structured path toward financial prosperity. Financial professionals provide more than help; they offer a roadmap personalized to your needs and dreams.

Beyond just the numbers, these professionals can provide emotional support. They understand the anxieties tied to money, the concerns about future uncertainties, and people's aspirations. They can become allies, supporting your financial journey, celebrating successes, and providing counsel during challenges.

The realm of finance, with its varied pathways and potential pitfalls, is one where guidance is beneficial and often essential.

Financial professionals who are also educators can stand as lighthouses in this vast sea, illuminating the way, helping avoid obstacles, and helping to ensure the journey toward financial well-being is prosperous and serene.

Carla's life moved to a place of confidence and clarity from uncertainty and confusion. Her story is a powerful reminder that we don't need to walk alone in the financial growth journey. With trust and financial professionals' expertise, they can light the way.

"

Without counsel plans fail, but with many advisers they succeed.

PROVERBS 15:22

CHAPTER 13

The Way Forward

A Vision for a Financially Literate Future

Our journey to financial literacy reflects a picture of urgent need but also one of hope...

The pages of history and contemporary stories show the highs and lows of financial education. But as we conclude this exploration, we must cast our gaze forward. What does the future hold for financial literacy in America? More importantly, what can it hold?

Imagine an America where every child, upon entering school, could be guaranteed lessons in mathematics, science, literature, and a solid foundation in financial literacy. Imagine teenagers graduating high school with dreams of college or a career and a clear understanding of credit scores, the importance of savings, and the basics of investing.

Envision young adults stepping into the world, not fearful of the looming specter of student loans but equipped with the knowledge to manage them. Picture families planning vacations not based on current whims but on well-structured budgets and financial plans, ensuring fun without financial fallout. Visualize financial institutions designing products that foster wealth accumulation for all their clients instead of offering credit cards that take advantage of uninformed borrowers.

This vision is about taking control, giving everyone the tools to lead lives of security, prosperity, and confidence.

Nora Ephron captured this when she said,

"Your education is a dress rehearsal for a life that is yours to lead."

Proper Education Prepares Us For Life

And in today's world, what's more foundational to life than understanding, managing, and growing your finances?

The ripples of this vision don't stop at individuals. A financially literate population contributes more effectively to the economy. They make better consumers, understanding the value of their purchases. They make more informed decisions, adding to market stability. The socio-economic repercussions are far-reaching. Reduced debt means less stress on families, leading to healthier communities. The positive cycle continues, with better financial decisions leading to more significant opportunities, better health, and increased community participation.

But how do we achieve this vision? It starts with a commitment by all of us. It begins by recognizing that financial literacy is as fundamental a right as any other form of education by making it part of our school curriculums, making it a community focus, ensuring that media and technology platforms prioritize spreading this knowledge, and continually advocating for its importance.

It also calls for collaboration:

- Financial Professionals
- Community Leaders
- Educators
- Parents
- Everyone has a role...

Bringing this vision to life calls for building bridges between all groups, to help ensure that the knowledge flow is seamless, current, and accessible.

As this book comes to a close, let's not see it as an end but as a beginning—a starting point for discussions, reforms, and transformations. Every lesson absorbed, every strategy applied, and every individual empowered through financial literacy brightens our country's prospects.

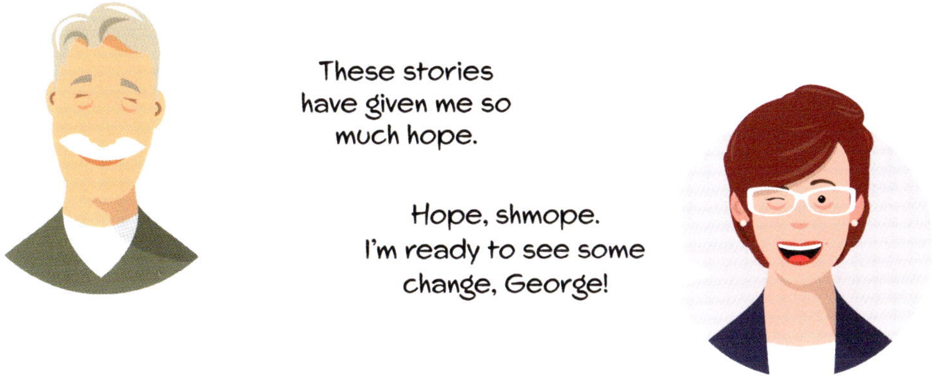

In the face of challenges, as we chart our course forward, we must remember that financial literacy is a movement, a right, and a foundation for a stronger future. As we march forward, remember that every step toward financial literacy isn't just a step toward personal prosperity. It's a stride towards a brighter, more resilient, and more prosperous America.

As Michael Jackson said in his song, Man in the Mirror,

> “
>
> **If you want to make the world a better place, take a look at yourself, and then make a change.**

Such advice is ever so appropriate in our pursuit of financial literacy. It starts with us. It begins with a willingness to learn, change, and make better financial decisions. With this mindset, we can collectively shape a more financially literate America.

Next Steps

Your Financial Empowerment Awaits

Bravo! You've just completed a transformative first phase in revolutionizing your financial journey—one you may have been putting off for quite some time.

This exploration of financial literacy is about claiming a future of possibilities and potential. As the seasons of life transition and challenges arise, it's paramount to keep building on this financial foundation, ensuring you're always prepared.

Armed with knowledge, you now have all the necessary equipment to climb the mountain. But remember, passion without action is potential unfulfilled. Grabbing your compass, leaving the base camp, and climbing upwards on your financial journey to leverage the wisdom you've garnered is vital.

Along with the 7 Money Milestones® from our other books in TheMoneyBooks Series, take these action steps:

Talk About Money
Speak openly about finances with your loved ones, breaking age-old silences.

Know Your Financial Situation
Periodically take stock of your cash flow, assets, insurance, and debts.

Eliminate The Unnecessary
Ward off needless fees, high-interest debts, and unproductive financial habits.

Set Your Financial Goals
Establish short, medium, and long-term financial objectives.

Make a Plan
Design a pragmatic financial strategy and budget. Commitment is where change happens.

Save and Invest More Money
Understand that every small saving or investment counts. Consistency is the magic ingredient.

For readers of our book series, here's some essential guidance:

Forge an Alliance with a Financial Professional
Engage a trusted financial professional to get strategic direction tailored to your unique circumstances. They can be the compass guiding your journey.

Be the Beacon
Light someone else's path with your newfound knowledge. Initiate money talks with peers, families, or associates. Foster a community where finance isn't a taboo but a shared quest.

Financial fortitude isn't achieved overnight. It's the culmination of consistent, informed actions. And while the road might be long, each step you take carves a path to prosperity and peace of mind. With your newly acquired insights, the horizon of financial freedom isn't just a dream—it's a destination.

"

Too many people spend money they haven't earned, to buy things they don't want, to impress people they don't like.

- WILL ROGERS

You're reading It!

Share this ebook with someone who needs it.

Request a copy from one of our Financial Educators.

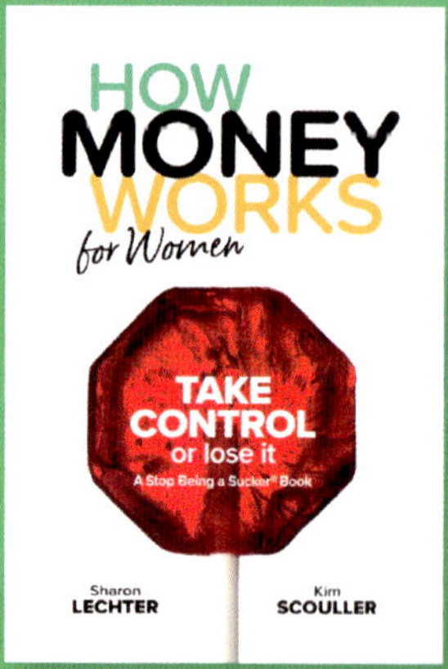

Request a copy from one of our Financial Educators.

Request a copy of each of our books from your financial educator.

Start Your Financial Odyssey With Our Books and Courses in TheMoneyBooks Series

Now, having learned more about the need for financial literacy and understanding its importance, you stand at a pivotal juncture. Knowledge, as powerful as it is, is just a tool. A tool that, if left unused, rusts away, losing its potential to bring about change. Education without action is like an unlit lamp, holding the potential to shine brightly in a dark room.

Our books, *HowMoneyWorks: Stop Being a Sucker* and *HowMoneyWorks for Women: Take Control or Lose It*, await you with strategies, insights, and tools to further illuminate your path. They are not just books but compasses designed to guide you through the intricate maze of personal finance, helping you avoid pitfalls and seize opportunities.

Reading alone won't carve your path to financial freedom. It's imperative to apply that knowledge into concrete actions.

Consider attending one of our financial literacy courses, either in person or via Zoom. Immerse yourself in interactive sessions, ask questions, challenge your preconceptions, and sharpen your skills. These courses are a meeting of people just like you who want to take control of their finances.

Every individual's financial journey is unique. You'll need a guide to customize this knowledge to your story and mold it into a blueprint for your dreams and aspirations.

Seek out a trusted financial professional. Together, assess where you stand today.

Then, envision where you wish to be and chart out a course. Their expertise, combined with your newfound knowledge, can be the potent duo that brings your financial dreams to life.

As you stand at this threshold, ready to step into a future of clarity, stability, and growth, remember this:

Time is your most valuable currency. Each passing moment is an opportunity. The time you squander today is the time your money can never reclaim.

So, harness the power of now. Don't let inertia be the anchor that drags down your dreams.

Let your journey into TheMoneyBooks universe be the catalyst for change. Let the lessons you've learned be the wind beneath your wings. And let your actions today be the stepping stones towards a financially liberated tomorrow.

Education has lit the torch. Now, it's up to you to carry it forward, illuminating your path and those of others.

Your brighter, more informed financial future is waiting.

About the Authors

Tom Mathews

Tom is from Cincinnati, Ohio, and graduated from St. Xavier High School and Xavier University, both esteemed Jesuit institutions. In addition to earning a degree in accounting, he fostered an enduring love for music and playing the trumpet, passions he continues to pursue to this day.

He has offices and leaders across the U.S., Canada, and Puerto Rico. His teams are highly regarded for their professionalism and consistent growth. A frequent member of corporate councils and boards, Tom has been at the forefront of driving marketing initiatives throughout his career.

One of the seven co-founders of World Financial Group, Tom serves as the driving force behind WealthWave as its founder and CEO. A Certified Financial Educator® with over four decades of experience in the financial services industry, Tom has consistently been at the forefront of innovation. Notable accomplishments include pioneering the first corporate website in the financial industry in 1993 and championing the integration of laptops into mainstream corporate culture.

Tom co-authored the book *Aim For The Heart: Leading to Build Great Teams* alongside Mac Anderson, the visionary behind Successories. In furtherance of his advocacy for financial literacy, Tom wrote *HowMoneyWorks: Stop Being a Sucker,* which has become a leading guide in personal finance since 2019. Through a combination of online and live courses, this book has shed light on financial knowledge and has garnered significant media attention, with over 350 features on TV, radio, and the web, including ABC, CBS, FOX, NBC, SiriusXM, *Newsweek,* and *The Wall Street Journal.*

Currently, Tom devotes his energy to public speaking, writing, creating training environments, and driving the growth of WealthWave. He is also behind LeadershipLIVE events and LeadershipNOW podcasts, and hosts VIP Green Carpet Day team-building initiatives on WealthWaveTV.

Tom and his wife, Cindy, reside near their daughters and grandchildren in Alpharetta, Georgia.

To reach Tom, you can email him at tom@wealthwave.com

tommathews.com • wealthwave.com/tom • howmoneyworks.com/tom • e2emakethemove.com/tom • youtube.com/wealthwave • @howmoneyworksofficial

Tom Mathews is a registered representative and investment advisor representative of Transamerica Financial Advisors, Inc. (TFA). WealthWave Media (WWM) is separate from and is not affiliated in any way with TFA. This book was written by Tom under an agreement with WWM and not as a representative of TFA. This book was published by and is owned by WWM.

Kim Scouller

Kim, a Louisville, Kentucky native, is recognized as an advocate for women and their finances. She has been an attorney for more than 30 years and served as in-house counsel for one of the largest financial services companies in the world.

While at Transamerica, she served in several executive roles for the company's insurance affiliates, broker-dealers, mutual funds, and investment advisors. In her last four years there, she served as the president of the Transamerica broker-dealer with the largest number of registered representatives.

As one of the few women broker-dealer presidents in the U.S., she traveled around the country talking with people, especially women, about the steps to identify and achieve their financial goals.

Wanting more control over her time, Kim left her corporate career to start her own financial business and law firm in Atlanta. A Certified Financial Educator®, Kim continues to speak with women about the importance and impact of financial education that leads to literacy.

Further cementing her financial literacy advocacy, Kim co-authored *HowMoneyWorks For Women: Take Control or Lose It,* a leading personal finance guide for women since 2023. Its online and live courses are enlightening multitudes on financial knowledge. Kim and her family live in Alpharetta, Georgia.

Kim can be reached at kim@wealthwave.com

wealthwave.com/kim • howmoneyworks.com/kim • e2emakethemove.com/kim

About the Authors (Continued)

Andy Horner

Andy is a Virginia native, and is a multifaceted leader known for his dynamic marketing and innovation skills. Andy has been instrumental in steering WealthWave to significant milestones, leveraging his deep understanding of marketing and industry trends. His vision is driven by a commitment to excellence and a passion for delivering value to clients.

Andy holds the dual roles of Chief Marketing Officer and Chief Technology Officer with WealthWave. In these capacities, he combines his marketing prowess with technological insights to drive the company's strategic direction.

Andy's expertise lies in bridging the gap between technology and business, ensuring that both dimensions align seamlessly to deliver optimal results.

Andy was also co-author of *HowMoneyWorks: Stop Being a Sucker.* His editing, design, and development of the characters featured in TheMoneyBooks series made it one of the top-selling personal finance books since 2019.

Throughout his career, Andy has demonstrated a knack for visionary thinking and a hands-on approach to problem solving. His leadership style is characterized by a focus on collaboration, innovation, and continuous growth. As he navigates his journey with WealthWave, Andy continues to leave an indelible mark on the financial industry, inspiring peers and fostering a culture of excellence.

Andy and his wife, Tonia, live in Cumming, Georgia, with their sons.

Andy can be reached at andy@wealthwave.com

Resources

1. TIAA Institute, "Financial well-being and literacy in a high-inflation environment: The 2023 TIAA Institute – GFLEC Personal Finance Index," Paul J. Yakoboski, Annamaria Lusardi, and Andrea Hasler (2023).
https://gflec.org/wp-content/uploads/2023/04/2023-P-Fin-Index-report-TIAA-Inst-and-GFLEC-Apr-2023.pdf

2. nerdwallet, "Most Americans Have a Monthly Budget, But Many Still Overspend," Andrew Marder (May 30, 2023).
https://www.nerdwallet.com/article/finance/data-2023-budgeting-report

3. Fortune, "'Turbulence ahead': Nearly 4 in 10 Americans lack enough money to cover a $400 emergency expense, Fed survey shows," Will Daniel (May 23, 2023).
https://fortune.com/2023/05/23/inflation-economy-consumer-finances-americans-cant-cover-emergency-expense-federal-reserve/

4. Next Gen Personal Finance, "Live U.S. Dashboard: Guarantee States," (2024).
https://www.ngpf.org/live-us-dashboard/

5. American Public Education Foundation, "The Nation's Report Card: Empowering Tomorrow's Generation, The Third Edition," (2024).
https://www.thenationsreportcard.org

6. NBC News, "More Americans are so worried about money, it's hurting their mental health," Rob Wile (May 9, 2023).
https://www.nbcnews.com/business/consumer/financial-wealth-and-mental-health-americans-worried-about-money-rcna83569#

What Other Leaders are Saying

Lacking financial literacy leaves us vulnerable, like an unlocked door allowing the financial industry to snatch away our American Dream.

– James Schwartz

Investing in knowledge pays the best interest.

– Benjamin Franklin

The cost of ignorance is far higher than the cost of education.

– Robin Bundy

Education is the most powerful weapon you can use to change the world.

– Nelson Mandela

True wealth lies not in the accumulation of money, but in the abundance of possibilities it can afford.

– Hanna Horenstein

A trusted financial professional can be like a compass in the turbulent sea of financial decisions.

– Matt Luckey

The best time to plant a tree was 20 years ago. The second best time is now.

– Chinese Proverb

Do not save what is left after spending, but spend what is left after saving.

– Warren Buffett

It's not how much money you make, but how much money you keep and how hard it works for you.

– Tom Mathews, Sr., CPA

A budget is telling your money where to go instead of wondering where it went.

– Dave Ramsey

Wealth consists not in having great possessions, but in having few wants.

– Epictetus

The only thing we must determine is how to make the most of the time we are given.

– Noelle Kim

Education is a priceless gem that accompanies us wherever we go.

– James Wilkerson

You can't enjoy the destination of financial freedom until you have the knowledge to light the path. Let financial literacy be your guide.

– Guillermo Milord